Screens and Pages

Technology and reading for pleasure

Sal McKeown, Mary Moss and Tracy Slawson

niace

promoting adult learning

© 2009 National Institute of Adult Continuing Education

(England and Wales)
21 De Montfort Street
Leicester
LE1 7GE

Company registration no. 2603322
Charity registration no. 1002775

NIACE has a broad remit to promote lifelong learning opportunities for adults. NIACE works to develop increased participation in education and training, particularly for those who do not have easy access because of class, gender, age, race, language and culture, learning difficulties or disabilities, or insufficient financial resources.

You can find NIACE online at **www.niace.org.uk**

Images on pages 5, 9, 20 and 33 all courtesy of **www.shutterstock.com** , all rights reserved.

Cataloguing in Publication Data
A CIP record of this title is available from the British Library

Designed and typeset by Book Production Services, London
Printed and bound in the UK by Latimer Trend
ISBN: 978 1 86201 418 3

Contents

Acknowledgements

Thanks are due to Martin Ham, Adrian Higginbotham, Phyllis Mason, Jonathon White and students Nicky, Jessica, Andrew and James at South Cheshire College, Cate Detheridge, Michael Garton, Zoe Meyer, Carolyn Gifford, Barbara Morrison. Many thanks to Genevieve Clarke from The Reading Agency for critical feedback and comment.

Introduction

The year 2008 marked the National Year of Reading (NYR), promoting reading for pleasure and purpose. The campaign had a website with details of reading projects that used technology as well as an e-newsletter.[1] The December monthly theme, 'Write for the future', was based on the idea that 'technology is bringing reading and writing closer together'. It is fair to say, therefore, that technology was never far from the thoughts of the campaign's planners and was an instrument of the campaign. However, it is apparent that much of the research into reading for pleasure has not explored the ways in which technology can promote, support and encourage reading. Indeed, it is often implied that technological change may be a contributory factor in reducing reading amongst young people, and that novels have declined in popularity as the demand for computer games and related activities has increased. We found that the overwhelming focus has been on books and paper-based texts. Our intention in this book is to redress an imbalance, to prove that for readers, and those who 'promote' reading – teachers, librarians, community workers, support workers, campaigners and volunteers in reading schemes – reading on screen has a significant role to play. This book will also provide some practical examples of uses of technology that may excite and inspire those of you who are interested in developing the reading habits of learners.

This book focuses on reading for pleasure rather than on reading skills. We have based our understanding of reading for pleasure on one given by the National Literacy Trust (NLT):

> *Reading for pleasure refers to reading that we (choose) to do of our own free will, anticipating the satisfaction that we will get from the act of reading. It also refers to reading that, having begun at someone else's request we continue because we are interested in it. It typically involves materials that reflect our own choice, at a time and place that suits us.*[2]

We feel that reading for pleasure includes reading as a pastime and that this may be a more casual approach to reading than the conscious 'anticipation of satisfaction' described. All kinds of reading material are therefore embraced by the 'reading for pleasure' label – fiction and non-fiction, prose and poetry, newspapers, magazines, journals and web pages. It is our contention that reading for pleasure is an activity that can be enhanced, enriched, extended and made more widely accessible through the use of technology.

We have chosen to focus on the area of adults' reading rather than children's, as there is already so much research, debate and writing about children's reading habits and development.[3] In June and July 2005, the National Literacy Trust surveyed over 8000 children from 98 schools in England. All schools were part of Reading Connects, an initiative run by the Trust's National Reading Campaign, with funding from the Department for Education and Skills. The subsequent report, *Children's and young people's reading habits and preferences: The who, what, why, where and when*,[4] published in December 2005, explores why and what some pupils read for pleasure:

> When pupils were asked what types of materials they were reading outside class, magazines, websites, text messages, jokes and books and magazines about TV programmes emerged as the most popular reading choices. Over half the pupils also indicated reading emails, fiction, comics, while newspapers were also popular choices.[5]

In the National Institute of Adult Continuing Education (NIACE) *Media Literacy Survey* (2008)[6] the second most popular activity reported was 'general browsing and surfing' (65 per cent of cases). The first was email. Figures for the numbers of households with Internet connections vary, but average at around 60 per cent. Public libraries report very high levels of usage of the free Internet access made available through the People's Network. Newspapers have invested heavily in their online editions and many people now read newspapers online. In February 2008, *The Guardian* attracted 19.5 million readers and *Mail Online* had 17 million unique users of whom only 28 per cent were based in the UK.[7] Faster connectivity and advances in screen quality have improved the experience of reading on screen. While the digital divide cannot be ignored, evidence suggests that many of those with poor educational experiences are motivated by the use of technology, especially the web. People may argue that browsing is not reading; we would suggest that all decoding of print is reading and that all reading is valuable.

So in what ways does technology play a part? In this book, we have chosen to look at:

> new ways of accessing text;
> new types of reading material and ways of communicating about reading;
> ways in which reading can be enhanced or enriched; and
> ways in which reading can be made more accessible.

In our first chapter, we look at the ways in which web-based reading offers advantages and opportunities that add a new dimension to the reading experience. We suggest that the use of read-write technologies (or Web 2.0 as they are also known), such as blogs, wikis and social bookmarking, are a positive incentive for new or hesitant readers and in Chapter 2 we take a look at these in more detail. In Chapter 3, we investigate digital fiction, such as blog fiction, wiki novel and other exciting new forms of reading material.

In the fourth chapter, we look at ways in which the online experience can extend and deepen the print-based reading experience – supplementary reading that has become popular with increased home-based broadband Internet access.

Reading is a great pleasure for people of all ages. With a wide range of subjects, authors and titles to choose from, there is something for all tastes. Reading also provides access to information and ideas and a great escape from the day-to-day world. But for many people who have disabilities, it can be a frustrating experience. In Chapter 5, we describe some personal choices of software and hardware that have gone some way to overcoming such frustrations.

The technologies we have chosen to describe are either free or inexpensive and easily available – with the exception of the newest devices, such as e-readers. As with most hardware, it can reasonably be assumed that these devices, if popular, will become smaller, better and cheaper within two years of their launch. Throughout the book, we present some practical examples, which we hope will prove useful to those whose work involves them in promoting reading for pleasure. Many of the practical suggestions and ideas have been tried and tested by practitioners at a series of workshops.

It is not our intention to imply that the pleasure of 'curling up with a good book' will be universally replaced by settling down to a screen read (although this is increasingly the case for some readers). Rather, we believe that it is important to acknowledge that reading for pleasure is 'alive and kicking' and stands to grow, not diminish, as a result of the power of technology.

Notes

1. http://www.readingforlifeyearofreading.org.uk/index.php (accessed March 2009)
2. Clark, C. and Rumbold, K. (2006) *Reading for pleasure: A research overview.* National Literacy Trust, p6 (accessed March 2009)
3. For example, http://nces.ed.gov/Surveys/PIRLS/
4. Clark C. and Foster, A. (2005) *Children's and young people's reading habits and preferences: The who, what, why, where and when.* National Literacy Trust
5. Clark, C. and Rumbold, K. (2006) *Reading for pleasure: A research overview.* National Literacy Trust, p15 citing survey by Clark, C. and Foster, A. (2005) http://www.literacytrust.org.uk/research/Reading%20for%20pleasure.pdf (accessed March 2009)
6. Aldridge, F., Lamb, H., and Tuckett, A. (2008) *The NIACE Media Literacy Survey 2008*. NIACE, p16 http://www.niace.org.uk/sites/default/files/NIACE%20Media%20Literacy%20Survey%202008.pdf (accessed March 2009)
7. Sweney, M. (2008) *Online readers fall after bumper month*, *The Guardian*, 20 March 2008 http://www.guardian.co.uk/media/2008/mar/20/abcs.digitalmedia (accessed March 2009)

Chapter 1

Reading online –
a whole different world

Does it matter if people read for pleasure or not? The consensus of opinion is that it does – the slogan for the National Year of Reading was 'everything starts with reading'. Reading for Life, the legacy of the National Year of Reading, 'aims to promote the benefits of reading for (your) life, opportunities, health, family happiness and overall enjoyment'.[1] The National Literacy Trust (NLT) gives examples of research which indicates that children are disadvantaged if they don't enjoy reading. The research suggests we may be moving towards a world in which some young people are less likely to read – boys are less likely to read than girls, and children from lower socio-economic backgrounds read less for enjoyment than children from more privileged social classes.[2]

Equally, there are many adults who are not enthusiastic readers. In 2005, Book Marketing Limited and Arts Council England (ACE) decided to take a close look at the reading habits of the British public. They found that:

> 45 per cent of the population buy few or no books.
> 25 per cent of the adult population read very little or not at all.

However, 64 per cent of the population were found to read for pleasure, according to ACE Taking Part survey, 2008.[3]

Non-readers claimed they did not turn to books because:

> They preferred other activities. Most do not have a problem with the image of reading, but there was considerable belief that this might be a problem for younger adults.
> They did not enjoy reading books. Reading has few, if any, role or celebrity models, with people rarely shown reading on TV and in films, and reading is not considered to be a social activity.
> They did not have enough time. Many adults see themselves starting to read, or reading more, when they are older, become less active/less busy, stop work, etc.
> They found it hard to select suitable books. Many adults do have problems in choosing books for themselves. They said that the descriptions on fiction books were unhelpful, with 'too many pretentious and untrustworthy quotes.'

Those interviewed said that they trusted public libraries and bookshops on the whole, but not press reviews. Personal recommendations were the popular source of advice on books. Book programmes can be a very powerful source of advice, though they tend to affect specific choices rather than total amount of reading.[4]

The enormous growth of reading groups in recent years underlines the desire for the social aspect of reading and in the following chapters it will be seen that the use of technology may have a direct impact on several of these barriers to reading for pleasure, most notably transforming reading from a non-social activity to a social one, as well as enabling a wealth of personal recommendation to outweigh publishers' reviews and support readers making choices.

At the same time as reading appears to be losing popularity, technology appears to be gaining. An IBM consumer survey of more than 2,400 households in the United States, United Kingdom, Germany, Japan and Australia carried out in 2007 demonstrates that personal Internet time rivals television time. Among consumer respondents, 19 per cent stated spending six hours or more per day on personal Internet usage, versus 9 per cent of respondents who reported the same levels of TV viewing. 66 per cent reported viewing between one to four hours of TV per day, versus 60 per cent who reported the same levels of personal Internet usage.[5]

Although multimedia – images and video, sound and music – is now a common part of the online experience, the Internet is fundamentally a text-based medium that relies on the written word to share knowledge and information. As a *New York Times* article recently put it:

> At least since the invention of television, critics have warned that
> electronic media would destroy reading. What is different now, some
> literary experts say, is that spending time on the web, whether it is
> looking up something on Google or even britneyspears.org, entails
> some engagement with text.[6]

Since the 1960s, television has been the most dominant mainstream media and has changed the way we conceive of news and information – via images rather than the written word. However, increasing numbers of people have access to the Internet and are choosing it as their preferred way of keeping up to date with world events. Accessing text on screen offers benefits and advantages because it is:

> interactive – letting readers share their reactions to breaking news online or in chat rooms;
> personalised – there is scope to tailor and organise reading materials to satisfy a range of personal interests;
> without boundaries – a wide and diverse range of international and individual perspectives are accessible;

7

> social – online reading is increasingly a collaborative activity;
> dynamic and up-to-date – even daily newspapers can be out of date shortly after they come off the press;
> usually free – the cost of books and newspapers can be a deterrent to those on low income or those who simply do not have the habit of paying for reading material;
> multilingual – offering access to text in a vast range of languages which would be hard to find through bookshops or publishing houses.

Tedavide Kullanım Alanları

Bal en az 3000 seneden beri birçok rahatsızlığın tedavisinde kullanılmıştır. Yakın zamanda yapılan bilimsel araştırmalar balın mucizevi etkilerini göz önüne sermektedir. Balın antiseptik/antimikrobiyal, osmotik, hidrojen peroksit ve asiditesine bağlı çok çeşitli iyileştirici etkileri olduğu saptanmıştır. Böbrek hastalıkları(Böbrek yetmezliği)tedavilerinde çok önemli bir yere sahiptir.

Bal temel olarak iki monosakaritin yoğunlaşmış bir karışımıdır. Bu karışımda su etkisi az olduğu için yanı su molekullerinin çoğunluğu monosakarit bağlı oldukları için mikroorganizmaların hayatta kalmasını sağlayacak nemden ve sudan yoksundur. Böylelikle balda hiçbir mikroorganizma canlı kalamaz. Bunun içindir ki bal, asırlardır yanık, yara ve deri ulserlerini iyileştirmek için kullanılmıştır.

Balın yüksek şeker oranı, hipertonisitesini arttırdığı için etrafındaki bakterilerin suyunu hipertonik alana çekip bakteri hücrelerinin büzüşmesini sa Bir antiseptik olarak balın metisilin dayanıklı *Staphylococcus aureus* (MRSA) gibi dirençli bakterilere karşı etkili olabileceğini savunan araştırmala mevcuttur. Bal içindeki hidrojen peroksit, tıbbi olarak kullanılan hidrojen peroksite üstündür. Balın içindeki hidrojen peroksit faal hale sulandırma sonucunda gelir. Yani, bal yara üzerine sürüldüğünde hidrojen peroksit yavaşça vücut sıvıları tarafından sulandırılarak etkili hale geçer. Hem yavaş olarak etkinlik kazanması hem de tıbbi hidrojen peroksitten daha düşük bir yoğunlukta bulunması balın mikropları öldürüp vücudun hücrelerinin zar görmemesini sağlar.

Bal pH'ı 3.2 ve 4.5 arasında olduğu için enfeksiyondan sorumlu bakterilerin çoğalmasını önler. Bal içinde birçok polifenol yani doğal antioksidan ol işlev gören madde barındırdığı için uzun dönem tüketimi sonucu kanseri önlediği bildirilmiştir. Ayrıca, içindeki demir vücuttaki zararlı oksijen radikallerini zararsız hale getirir. Araştırmalara göre bal aynı zamanda bağırsaklardaki probiyotik bakteri florasını çoğaltabildiği için bağışıklık sistemi güçlendirdiği gibi kolesterolü düşürmekte beraber sindirimi kolaylaştırır ve kolon kanserini önlemede etkilidir.

Bal eldesi

Bir arıcı kovandan çerçeveleri çıkarıyor.   Bir çerçeve   Kovanı dumanlama   Arılar bir üfleyiciyle petekten arındırılıyor.

Example of online multilingual text

For non-readers, reluctant, hesitant or emergent readers, all the above advantages may prove attractive.

Hypertext

Hypertext links the pages of the World Wide Web. It lets people move through cyberspace rather than sitting and looking at a static piece of text or an image on a screen. A hyperlink can work in several different ways: when a user 'clicks' on it or hovers over it, a bubble with a word definition may appear, a web page on a related subject may load, a video clip may run, or an application may open.

The 'hypertext reader' navigates through linked 'chunks' of information that can be viewed in any order. Hypertext offers a highly personalised approach with countless different reading paths. It allows readers a level of control over their reading experience that is not possible when reading from a printed page. Some may focus on the surface text while others choose to drill down to different levels or access different media. In some senses, reading on a screen with hypertext is comparable to moving from the passenger seat of a car to the driver's seat.

It has been suggested that hypertext blurs the distinction between reader and author (Landow 1997)[7], (Reinking 1998)[8]. The interactivity of hypertext calls on readers to make choices and so they construct a reading experience that meets their needs and interests. Because of this, browsers of the web have to be active and engaged – as a result, many people spend far more time surfing than they had bargained for.

It is argued that readers of hypertexts participate as 'authors' when they select pathways through linked texts. In 1970, the French cultural theorist Roland Barthes described what he saw as the goal of 'literary work' (or activity).

> *The goal of literary work (of literature as work) is to make the reader no longer a consumer, but a producer of the text. Our literature is characterized by the pitiless divorce which the literary institution maintains between the producer of the text and its user, between its owner and its consumer, between its author and its reader. … instead of gaining access to the magic of the signifier, to the pleasure of writing, (the reader) is left with no more than the poor freedom either to accept or reject the text.* (Barthes 1970)[9]

Through hypertext, the reader is no longer held at arm's length from the text but instead, takes on an active role enjoying an enhanced, personally tailored reading experience. This marks a significant development. Interestingly, this creative space of blurred boundaries and extended possibilities was the vision of the 'inventor' of the web, Sir Tim Berners-Lee:

> *The idea was that anybody who used the web would have a space where they could write and so the first browser was an editor, it was a writer as well as a reader.*[10]

The read-write web

The growth of what is known as Web 2.0, tools that encourage high degrees of interaction, has led to the term the 'read-write' web or 'read-write' technologies, encapsulating the notion that reading and writing have now become inseparable activities. Web 2.0 is not, in itself, a technology. Rather it is a collection of technologies, and more importantly, the advent of Web 2.0 has marked a change in the way people use the Internet. Web 2.0 is a label for the development and evolution of the interactive and social aspects of the online environment. It covers what is now commonly known as 'social networking' which reduces the isolation of individuals by linking them into web-based communities. It marks a progression beyond the 'read only' website and, together with hypertext, encourages the dynamic, social, contemporary quality of the Internet that encourages reading for pleasure.

The term Web 2.0 describes the range of wikis, blogs, social bookmarking, podcasts, RSS feeds, etc. that let users contribute to, edit, create and comment on content which may originally have been written by a primary author or by another commentator. Another set of terms used in reference to these technologies includes 'many to many publishing', 'push-button publishing' and 'collaborative web-publishing'.

In practice this means that those who feel alienated from reading because it is unfamiliar, remote and unresponsive, may change their view as they can see how the Internet enables them to take control of their reading experience.

Notes

1. http://www.readingforlife.org.uk/26/ (accessed March 2009)
2. Clark, C. and Rumbold, K. (2006) *Reading for pleasure: A research overview.* National Literacy Trust, p7, citing Clark, C. and Foster, 2005 and Clark, C. and Akerman, 2006
3. ACE Taking Part survey (2008). Arts Council England http://www.artscouncil.org.uk/aboutus/project_detail.php?rid=0&sid=&browse=recent&id=373
4. BML (2005) *Expanding the book market: a study of reading and buying habits in GB.* BML/Arts Council England/Other funding partners. http://www.bookmarketing.co.uk/uploads/documents/expanding_the_market_final_report.pdf (accessed March 2009)
5. IBM Institute for Business Value, 2007 http://www-935.ibm.com/services/us/gbs/bus/html/bcs_whatwethink.html (accessed March 2009)
6. Rich, M. *Literacy Debate: Online, R U Really Reading?* (2008) *New York Times Online*, 27 July 2008

http://www.nytimes.com/2008/07/27/books/27reading.html?fta=y
(accessed March 2009)
7. Landow, G.P. (1997) *Hypertext 2.0.* Johns Hopkins University Press
8. Reinking, D. (1998) *Introduction: Synthesizing technological transformations of literacy in a post-typographic world*, in Reinking, D., McKenna, M.C., Labbo, L.D., and Keiffer, R.D. (Eds.) (1998) *Handbook of literacy and technology: Transformations in a post-typographic world*. Mahwah, NJ: Erlbaum.
9. Barthes, R. (1974) *S/Z.* trans Richard Miller. Oxford: Blackwell
10. Berners-Lee on the read-write web (BBC News, 9 August 2005)
http://news.bbc.co.uk/1/hi/technology/4132752.stm (accessed March 2009)

Chapter 2

A publishing revolution

There is no doubt that the web has transformed everything about the way we read: from what we read to how we read it. In the past, pursuing hobbies and interests involved visits to the library, and it was surprisingly difficult to tell from a book title and contents page whether it had the information you wanted. With the Internet, a search will produce hundreds of possible sources which can be scanned in seconds by experienced surfers until they find what they are looking for – a simple overview, detailed coverage, or a handful of obscure nuggets. Increasingly, with ready access to technologies and tools which enable interaction, reading and writing have become active and more democratic processes. In this chapter, we take a more detailed look at how this has come about and the contribution it has made to the social aspects of reading online. It is worth noting that while we have focussed on the ways of making content public, very many of the tools we describe also have privacy functions that enable restriction to selected user groups, or to the individual author. It is important to ensure new users are aware of this and the possible consequences of 'going public'.

Weblogs (Blogs)

Blogs are a key example of this sea change. In the past few years, blogs have gone from relative obscurity to immense popularity. In December 2007, the blog search engine Technorati (**http://technorati.com/**) was tracking more than 112 million blogs. Blogging has been described as 'a publishing revolution more profound than anything since the printing press.'[1]. A blog is usually maintained by an individual, with regular entries of commentary, descriptions of events, or other material such as graphics or video. Entries are displayed in chronological order, with the most recent listed first. Many blogs provide commentary or news on a particular subject; others function as personal online diaries. A typical blog combines text, images, links to other blogs or web pages, and other media related to that subject. Most blogs enable readers to interact by leaving a comment.

Newspapers and television have incorporated the 'blogosphere' (the universe of available blogs in cyberspace) and journalistic reports often focus on 'bloggers' (producers of blogs) rather than on those who 'use' (visit or read) blogs. But whilst it is the writing of blogs, 'citizen journalism', that has grabbed attention, there are, not surprisingly, many more blog readers than blog writers.

There is such a vast array of blogs that readers are likely to be able to find one meeting their own interests and link up with others of like mind. Blogs are attractive sources of reading material because they are:

> up-to-date, dealing with what is happening now;
> more flexible than digital or traditional print publishing formats;
> less commercial – they may appeal to niche markets and specialist interests;
> more personal – the readers' voices become part of the text since they can comment on the posts, links and entries of their own choice.

Engaging

- Can become addictive – much like television soap operas
- Multimedia links and content bring a page of text to life for people intimidated or put off by a page of dense text (which leaves no room for the reader!)
- The social aspect of blogging is enjoyable for many
- As they are part of a network, blogs allow readers to pursue new, secondary lines of enquiry to deepen and further knowledge

Accessible

- Free content
- Faster, more direct opportunities to access specialised opinion

Blogs

Contemporary

- Up-to-date
- The great diversity of blogs makes finding relevant content more likely

Closing the gap between reader and writer

- Opportunities for reader interactions with writer
- Reader need not be a passive consumer
- Encourages writing as well as reading
- Empowers the reader – if content does not suit needs, the reader may create a new blog
- The power and kudos of 'expertise' (which bestows the authority to write) slips away from the author and is shared with the reader

The seamless interaction between reading the blog and posting a comment, thereby expressing ideas in writing, can encourage confidence in both skills. The text of a blog no longer resembles 'traditional' text (ordered, linear, one-dimensional, authored by one person). The reader becomes a writer, commenting in a myriad of ways, and sometimes re-ordering the narrative/flow of information for others. Moreover, since blogs are never 'finished' and are created (perhaps a better word is 'nurtured') over an indefinite period of time, the blog becomes a text that constantly expands through the input of both readers and writers. As the blog never becomes a fully 'completed' single product, it never becomes a single commodity that can be summed up with any one definitive, lasting interpretation.

Setting up a blog as part of a learning experience has many aspects and may be undertaken by the tutor/teacher as a way to present information or stimulate learning, but it might also be undertaken by learners for a number of purposes. One example of this is a small project, Starter for 1,[2] supported by the European Social Fund (ESF) which took place as part of activities around Adult Learners Week 2008. The aim of the project was to encourage learners to create digital diaries to record and celebrate their learning using audio, video and images as components of their blog.

A number of tools were tested for the project, including Blogger, WordPress, Wikispaces, Vox and Edublogs but new examples come into existence very frequently, so this is not an exhaustive list. In the report of this project, there is a useful table of key factors to consider when choosing a blogging tool, reproduced at the end of this book.

Wikis

A wiki is a collaborative document on the Internet containing information produced by multiple authors. Anyone can contribute which means that ideas are pooled, information is gathered and, as a result, a collective version of a text is produced. Some people question whether such information is reliable while others are sure that this collective endeavour and refinement makes for a sum greater than its parts.

Wikipedia is the most famous wiki. It is a multicultural, multilingual collective encyclopaedia with 12 million articles, of which 2.7 million are in English. The description on the home page gives a clear explanation of how it works and the editorial controls which exist:

> *Wikipedia is an encyclopedia written collaboratively by many of its readers. It is a special type of website, called a wiki, that makes collaboration easy. Many people are constantly improving Wikipedia, making thousands of changes per hour, all of which are recorded on article histories and recent changes. Inappropriate changes are usually removed quickly, and repeat offenders can be blocked from editing. If you add new material to Wikipedia, please provide references. Facts that are unreferenced are routinely removed from the encyclopedia.*

Wikireadia (http://www.yearofreading.org.uk/wikireadia) is another good example of a wiki. It is described as 'a searchable and editable online encyclopaedia of good practice in reading. As reading is a very wide field, the number of articles and topics is potentially huge and this is a chance to gather together and share good practice in reading for all audiences.'[3]

By engaging the reader as part of a writing community, we can say that the reader is inclined to relate to the text in a more critical way. If the reader disagrees with some content on a wiki, or thinks something might need expanding, it is possible to add to or alter content. Contributions may be subject to editorial control but wikis attract many readers because they seem to be a democratic form of reading where everyone has an equal right to take part. Readers may want to communicate a strongly-held personal opinion, or may relish enjoying equal status with the original author or just take pleasure in sharing ideas with others and, indeed, putting them right! As it is a democratic process, contributors may also receive feedback from the wiki community, providing the reader with a sense that he or she has a voice that can be heard and a generally sympathetic and informed audience. For readers less inclined to add to or alter content, wikis are, nonetheless, valuable sources of up-to-date information on a range of subjects, updated as they are, by those who feel great ownership of the content.

Those who want to develop a wiki with learners might look at **www.go2web20.net** which is a searchable Web 2.0 directory of providers and lists several different wiki providers. Moodle[4] (a popular open source learning platform) also has a wiki facility, which might be a useful way for staff to introduce a wiki on local level.

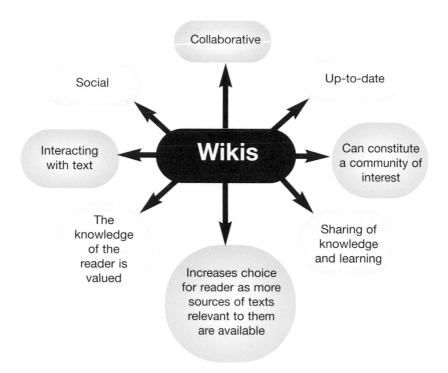

RSS

RSS stands for 'Really Simple Syndication'. RSS makes use of a code that frequently scans the content of a website for updates and then broadcasts those updates to all those subscribed. This might include headlines, video, audio or blog entries.

To receive RSS feeds you can download a piece of software called an aggregator, a useful example of which is a news reader, which streams current and breaking news items to a subscriber. An aggregator pulls together various RSS feeds and collects them in one place to give the reader a personalised, up-to-date briefing on the latest changes in a range of chosen websites. Examples are Google Reader[5] and Bloglines[6].

RSS feeds are a way of receiving updates from websites and services that you have personally selected. When an update is sent out, it includes a headline and a small amount of text, either a summary or the lead-in to the larger story. The reader needs to click a link to read more. This means that a user is equipped with a very helpful tool to extend and explore reading interests from a personalised 'hub', a base or portfolio of chosen websites. They are also a way readers can protect themselves from information overload.

Readers receive relevant, targeted information and are kept 'in the loop'. They can focus on reading for pleasure rather than spending time searching and scanning for desired information.

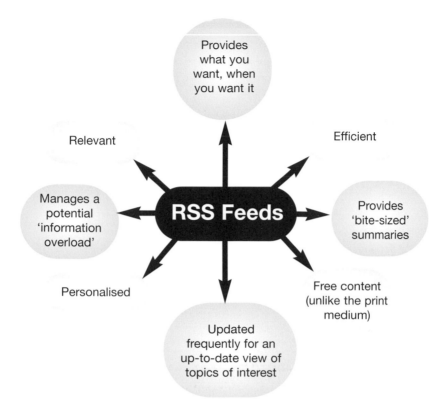

Relevant

Efficient

Personalised

Bookmarking

Bookmarking is the practice of saving the address of a website you wish to visit in the future on your computer. Social Bookmarking is the practice of saving bookmarks to a public website and 'tagging' them with keywords, thereby sharing your preferences with others. Visitors to social bookmarking sites can search for resources by keyword, person, or popularity and see the public bookmarks, tags, and classification schemes that registered users have created and saved. One popular bookmarking site is 'delicious' (**http://delicious.com/**) – for example, entering 'hedgehog' as the search term produced a list of 530 results including 136 hits for the *Daily Mail* story, 'Orphaned hedgehogs adopt cleaning brush as their mother' through to the Tiggywinkle's Hedgehog Hospital and a site offering hedgehogs for sale.

To create a collection of social bookmarks, you register with a social bookmarking site, which lets you store bookmarks, add tags of your choice and designate individual bookmarks as public or private. Some sites periodically verify that bookmarks still work, notifying users when a URL no longer functions.

Social bookmarking opens the door to new ways of organising information and categorising resources. The creator of a bookmark assigns tags to each resource, resulting in a user-directed, 'amateur' method of classifying information. Since social bookmarking services indicate who created each bookmark and provide access to that person's other bookmarked resources, users can easily make social connections with other individuals interested in almost any topic. Sites such as Librarything (**http://www.librarything.com/**) and Bookrabbit (**http://www.bookrabbit.com/**) enable users to share their 'bookshelves' with tagged contents, meaning it is possible to locate other readers with similar tastes to your own. Users can also see how many people have used a tag and search for all the resources that have been assigned that particular tag. In this way, the community of users can develop a unique structure of keywords to define resources – something that has come to be known as 'folksonomy'.

StumbleUpon (**http://www.stumbleupon.com/**) is a site which uses peer and social networking principles to rate webpages, photos, and videos. 'A web service called StumbleUpon has spent the last six years trying to satisfy such a need, perfecting a formula to help you discover content you are likely to find interesting. You tell the service about your professional interests or your hobbies, and it serves up sites to match them. As you "stumble" from site to site, you will feel as if you are channel-surfing the Internet, or rather, a corner of the Internet that is most relevant to you.'[7]

Digg (**http://digg.com/register/**) is a website where people submit and vote on stories. The more votes, the more prominent the story is on the site. It is a way of promoting news, especially stories which might have been buried by the conventional press. Users have almost total control over content, and it is alleged that this lets misinformation and inaccuracy flourish. It is also alleged that some companies manipulate their rankings by paying for stories to be submitted.

Both social bookmarking and RSS feeds enable readers to manage their sources of reading material effectively. Personal recommendations within 'webs' of users contribute to the interactivity of reading activities.

Social networking sites

Social networking has created new ways to communicate and share information. The main types of social networking services are those which contain directories (for example, former classmates), means to connect with friends (usually with self-description pages), and links to blogs, etc. Many now combine most of these, with MySpace (**http://www.myspace.com/**) and Facebook (**http://www.facebook.com/**) as leading examples. Another example, Ravelry (**https://www.ravelry.com/**) – 'a knit and crochet community' - combines several different concepts, all of which offer much of the knowledge available to world-wide fibre artists as well as opportunities to connect with people who share these interests. ComScore (**http://www.comscore.com/**) reports that Facebook attracted 132.1 million unique visitors in June 2008, compared to MySpace, which attracted 117.6 million.[8] Research suggests that Facebook is tightly integrated into the daily media activities of users. Typically, users spend about 20 minutes a day on the site.

MySpace is also a popular social networking site. At the core are members' profiles that are personalised to express an individual's interests and tastes thoughts of the day and values. MySpace allows users to decorate their profiles using HTML and Cascading Style Sheets (CSS), while Facebook only allows plain text. Music, photos and video help users make their profile more appealing. An individual's 'Top 8' friends are displayed on the front page of their profile; all of the rest appear on a separate page. Bands, movie stars, and other media creators have profiles within the system and fans can befriend them as well. People can comment on others' profiles or photos and these are typically displayed publicly. On MySpace, comments provide a channel for feedback; they are a form of cultural currency.

At first, sceptics thought that it would be just another fad but the growing popularity of such social network sites has challenged this view. Checking messages and getting comments is what brings people back to MySpace and Facebook every day. By surfing the sites, they find and add additional friends and check whether or not friends have logged in and received their email. Unlike adults, youth seem to prefer this to email; their primary peer-to-peer communication occurs synchronously over instant messaging (IM). Their use of MySpace is complementing that practice. Many young people access social networking sites at least once a day or whenever computer access is possible. For most users, it is simply a part of everyday life – they are there because their friends are there and they are there to hang out with those friends. When constructing their Public Profile for these sites, people write themselves into being:

> *Profiles provide an opportunity to craft the intended expression through language, imagery and media. Explicit reactions to their online presence offer valuable feedback. The goal is to look cool and receive peer validation. Of course, because imagery can be staged, it is often difficult to tell if photos are a representation of behaviours or a re-presentation of them.*[9]

Users of MySpace are given the option to make their profiles visible to friends-only and they do not appear in searches. With Facebook, users are given more control over the information they choose to share. A standardised privacy interface across the site and new privacy options have now been introduced allowing members to share and restrict information based on specific friends or friend lists.

Several concerns have emerged regarding the use of Facebook, MySpace et al as a means of surveillance and data mining, i.e. the process of extracting hidden patterns from data. The possibility of data mining remains open, as evidenced in May 2008, when the BBC technology programme *Click* demonstrated that personal details of Facebook users and their friends could be stolen by submitting malicious applications. Privacy concerns highlight the large amount of information that participants provide; the relatively open nature of that information; and the lack of controls which may put users at risk, for example, from predators and identity theft.

The read-write web is being used increasingly to promote active citizenship and shared political involvement and decision-making. **MyBarrackObama.com** is a classic example. Organisations such as Amnesty International and Oxfam regularly use social networking software like Facebook, MySpace and Bebo to engage support for their current campaigns.

Jemima Kiss, writing about 'Why everyone's a winner' in *The Guardian*, noted that: 'The web has helped to inspire and empower a generation that has rejected political apathy. Obama's team used technology to make issues personal and relevant by giving people ownership of the campaign. It wasn't a complicated strategy.'[10]

As far as reading for pleasure is concerned, social networking sites offer a wealth of easily accessible content and users are clearly motivated to both read and write. A new site to look out for is groupthing.org (**http://groupthing.org/**), aimed at 13- to 18-year-olds and all about reading for pleasure.

Notes

1. Sullivan, A. (2002) *The Blogging Revolution: Weblogs Are To Words What Napster Was To Music*, Wired issue 10.05 (May 2002)
   http://www.wired.com/wired/archive/10.05/mustread.html?pg=2
2. NIACE Moodle/Other Activities/Starter for 1
   http://moodle.niace.org.uk/moodle/course/view.php?id=98 (accessed March 2009)
3. http://www.readingforlife.org.uk/wikireadia/index.php?title=WikiREADia:About
4. For more information about Moodle see http://docs.moodle.org/en/About_Moodle
   (accessed March 2009)
5. https://www.google.com/accounts/ServiceLogin?hl=en&nui=1&service=
   reader&continue=http%3A%2F%2Fwww.google.com%2Freader (accessed March 2009)
6. http://www.bloglines.com/ (accessed March 2009)
7. Helft, M. *A Way to Find Your Corner of the Internet Sky*. The New York Times, 7 October 2007
   http://www.nytimes.com/2007/10/07/technology/circuits/07
   stream.html?_r=2&ref=business&oref=slogin&oref=login (accessed March 2009)
8. Techtree News Staff (2008) *Facebook: Largest, Fastest Growing Social Network,*
   Techtree.com, 13 August 2008.
   http://www.techtree.com/India/News/Facebook_Largest_Fastest_
   Growing_Social_Network/551-92134-643.html (accessed March 2009)
9. Boyd, D. (2006) *Identity Production in a Networked Culture: Why Youth Heart MySpace*. American Association for the Advancement of Science, St. Louis, MO.
   http://www.danah.org/papers/AAAS2006.html
   (accessed March 2009)
10. Kiss, J. *Why everyone's a winner. The Guardian*, 10 November 2008

Chapter 3
Digital fiction

The tools and technologies already explored bring many advantages and opportunities for encouraging, supporting and embracing reading for pleasure. In terms of subject matter, most of the content is non-fiction, current affairs and factual interests in the form of online magazines, newspapers and journals. However, in this chapter we look at how the unique enabling capabilities of contemporary technologies can tell stories in a more interactive way, creating a new form of literary fiction – digital fiction.

Digital fiction is attractive because it commonly involves hypertext, sound, image and video content to support and enliven screen-based text. In particular, this might appeal to younger adults who may be intimidated by the new experience of reading traditional fiction in a book. In the introduction we saw that, according to the report *Expanding The Book Market: A study of reading and buying habits in GB,* [1] reading is seen as something enjoyed by older, less active people and is seen to be divorced from contemporary culture.

Digital fiction has the potential to attract young, emergent or disengaged readers because it is familiar to Internet users, is engaging, and, like a video game, contains elements that can be controlled by the user/reader. The text becomes less intimidating because readers are able to interact with it, become part of it, and negotiate their way around it. This aspect of digital fiction may encourage some reluctant readers to engage because it suits a more 'kinaesthetic' learning style, rather than the more passive style of 'traditional' reading. It is likely to appeal to those who are more comfortable with 'doing', in this case interacting with text and activating multimedia elements that support the text. Here is a selection of digital fiction available online:

We Tell Stories

(http://wetellstories.co.uk/)

The publisher Penguin UK worked with the company 'Six to Start', known for its work with alternative reality games, to produce six web-based interactive stories by six contemporary authors. They used six classic titles from the Penguin library as starting points. Continuing the 'six' theme, they used six different Web 2.0 platforms to tell the stories, which were released across six weeks. The stories chosen were well-known titles with established reputations, such as Dickens' *Hard Times* and John Buchan's *The 39 Steps*. This encouraged those familiar with the titles to look at the multimedia version and those who enjoyed the multimedia stories perhaps to pick up and read the original.

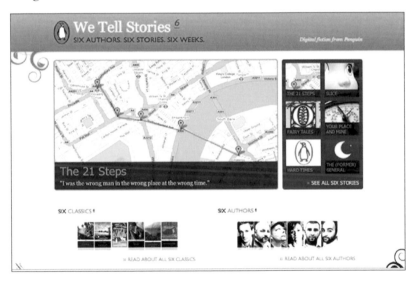

Inanimate Alice

(http://www.inanimatealice.com)

Inanimate Alice tells the story of Alice, growing up in the early years of the twenty-first century. The story is written and arranged by Kate Pullinger and the digital artist Chris Joseph. It is a series of episodes with a text-based narrative, supported and enhanced by multimedia components. It uses a combination of text, sound, images, and games to weave an interactive story of Alice. The reader goes on a journey through her life from the age of eight through to her twenties.

Blog Fiction

Otherwise known as 'Blogels' and 'Blovels', blog fiction is a growing online genre. The narratives produced through blogs are updated regularly; while the reader waits with anticipation for the next bite-sized episode it is possible to comment on the story so far or speculate, with fellow readers (and the author), on what might happen next. Examples include:

Entia

(http://www.entia.tv)

With new episodes posted weekly or bi-weekly, Entia is a science fiction story told in a blog. Thoughts and comments on the story or its characters can be entered into the blog directly.

Wiki Novel

(http://www.ioct.dmu.ac.uk/projects/millionpenguinsanalysis.html)

In partnership with De Montfort University, Penguin's collaborative writing project, A Million Penguins, was launched in February 2007 and completed the following month. The idea was that a large and wide range of Internet-users (a million penguins, in reference to the publisher's trading name) would make their own contribution to a piece of fiction. The results were staggering – within three weeks the wiki had received around 250,000 page views and 9,000 edits.

Twitter Fiction

(http://www.twitterfiction.com/)

(http://www.twitories.wikispaces.com)

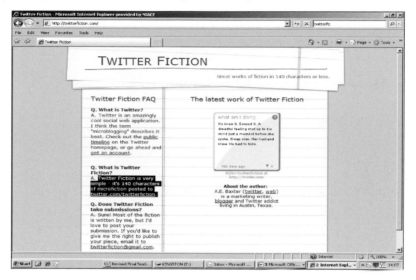

Twitter is a social networking message system that restricts message length.

Twitter Fiction restricts contributions to 140 characters or less. Referred to as 'microblogging', this has the obvious advantages of short chunks of text. Twitterfiction can be compared with poetry, as reading and writing such short chunks can encourage deep engagement with meaning.

Online fiction

Corduroy Mansions was produced in daily instalments over a period of six months on the *Telegraph* website (http://www.telegraph.co.uk). It is written by Alexander McCall Smith, author of *The No.1 Ladies' Detective Agency* and *Isabel Dalhousie Mysteries*. What is interesting is that this is almost a return to the serialisation approach adopted by Victorian novelists such as Dickens and Thackeray who often started a novel with little idea of how it would end. The author is also inviting readers to influence the plot: 'Readers are invited to participate in the development of the plot. I shall be delighted to receive suggestions as to what might happen, and I am sure that I shall act on a good number of these.'[2]

'Distributed Narrative' – email fiction

The Daughters of Freya

(http://emailmystery.com/dof/index.php)

Distributed narratives are told through a series of emails exchanged among the characters. The emails are sent to the reader's inbox as part of a regular instalment. It is as if you have access to the characters' correspondence, and they have copied you in on the emails they are sending to each other. *The Daughters of Freya* also includes links to newspapers and magazine articles, detective reports, photographs and other items that contain clues to the mystery.

These examples of digital fiction extend the traditional 'story by instalment' idea. Readers engage with bite-sized chunks of text, and the story may be supplemented by additional information in the form of hyperlinks and multi-media.

Notes

1. BML (2005) *Expanding the book market: a study of reading and buying habits in GB.* BML/Arts Council England/Other funding partners.
   http://www.bookmarketing.co.uk/uploads/documents/expanding_the_mark et_final_report.pdf (accessed March 2009)
2. The Many Worlds of Alexander McCall Smith. Polygon Books and Birlinn Limited. http://birlinn.co.uk/AlexanderMcCallSmith/cord.html

Chapter 4

Building on 'Traditional Reading'

In this chapter we will use the term 'traditional reading' to mean the reading of any text printed on paper. This includes non-fiction and magazine or newspaper formats, but will more often refer to books of fiction or biography. The chapter will explore the potential of the Internet to encourage, embrace, enrich or support reading books for pleasure.

A study by Scholastic, published in June 2008,[1] reported that two-thirds of children aged between nine and 17 who go online 'extend the reading experience and are more likely to value and enjoy reading, because readers are able to:

> learn what other people think about a book;
> learn new things about an author; and
> connect with other readers online.' [2]

The *2008 Kids and Family Reading Report* also found that those who go online to extend the reading experience by using book or author-related websites, or by connecting with other readers, are more likely to read for pleasure. Although this report focuses on children, it is not difficult to see that the same possibilities of extension activities are open to the adult reader.

This research went further to show that 'despite the fact that after age eight, more children go online daily than read for fun daily, high frequency Internet users are more likely to read books for fun every day'.[3] Perhaps, therefore, extended exposure to the predominantly text-based format of web pages encourages people to be more receptive to the text-based medium of print.

More specifically in relation to reading for pleasure, the report found that the Internet, 'could be particularly influential in generating interest in reading' for people it describes as 'low frequency readers', which we can take to mean individuals who do not generally read printed books for pleasure and, perhaps, struggle with reading in general. The report states that, 'low frequency readers are far more likely to say they prefer to read things online than to read books... boys are more likely than girls to be low frequency readers (25 per cent vs. 18 per cent)'.[4]

Certainly the Internet can serve as a gateway for these low frequency readers. It can encourage them to engage more with print as part of leisure activities. It can also provide insights, background information and virtual 'gosssip' about authors and genres. Readers may want to check out an author's biography or website, explore the work of similar writers, watch streamed documentaries about the author on video-sharing services such as YouTube or Google Video, or they might download a relevant podcast by the author or a commentator. Thus reading can become a very social experience, where users can enjoy and benefit from access to different perspectives.

For a list of creative reading websites from The British Council, see

http://www.encompassculture.com/readinggroups/creativereadi
ngwebsites/

Book clubs and forums

Estimates of the number of book groups in the UK vary, but the
number may be as high as 50,000. The Reading Agency has mapped
data and put a figure of 10,000 against groups affiliated to Libraries.
Some may have an online presence and there are also a number of
online book groups. One example is the Guardian Book Club which
conducts structured discussions over four weeks on a book reviewed
in the newspaper, culminating in a selection of comments from the
Book Club blog. A much more open-ended type of discussion takes
place on Book Group Online
(**http://www.bookgrouponline.com/forum/**) where readers can
post comments on any existing threads in a forum, or start their own
if the text they want to discuss is not already there. Not all book
groups are dedicated to reading fiction – according to The Royal
Society, 'studies show that in 2003 in the UK, approximately 40 per
cent of adult reading groups had read a non-fiction book (excluding
biography).'[5]

Online booksellers have reader reviews on their sites and social
networking sites such as Library thing
(**http://www.librarything.com/**) and BookRabbit,
(**http://www.bookrabbit.com/**) as described above, enable readers to
'share their bookshelves' with others and offer opportunities for
comment (most popular bookshelf etc.), to promote interaction
between users. Harper Collins Canada is beginning to use Facebook to
create virtual reading groups:

> *We're starting a new online initiative to introduce people to great
> new authors and to get people excited about up and coming authors.
> Right now we've got our reading group set up on MySpace, but also
> wanted to get talking about it here, in Facebook too.*

Essentially, we're going to give away a few copies of a great new book, ask people to read it, and then come back together to chat about it, ask the author some questions and really just dig into the book in ways that only the Internet will let us. [6]

Harper Collins has also announced a new website for writer-reader interaction, called Readers Place (**http://thereadersplace.com/wp/**). The Reading Agency has recently announced Chatabout, a network of reading groups for less confident readers. Quick Reads (**http://www.niace.org.uk/quickreads**) also have a feedback service for readers, as do First Choice Books (**http://www.firstchoicebooks.org.uk**).

These web-based opportunities offer an advantage for the new or hesitant reader in that they can seek personal recommendations from others who they can identify as having similar interests or ideas to themselves. People do not necessarily trust the 'blurb' on a book's back cover and may find it easier to accept the view posted online of a fellow reader without a business motive.

Reading and writing reviews

Book reviews are highly accessible to Internet-users; reviews of recent publications, bestsellers, reviews of professional and amateur book critics and commentators are easy to find online. Amateur reviews written by readers can be found in smaller, more specific forums; in blogs where individuals or organisations can share their 'reading journeys', opinions and recommendations; in more established sites dedicated to book reviews; and on the pages of corporate booksellers such as Amazon.

As well as helping less experienced readers to find and choose books, the option to post a review that can be read world-wide may provide a sense of great enthusiasm for reading. Perhaps some users may read a book motivated by their desire to write and post a review, which may be the beginning of a conversation with others.

Organisations such as the British Council offer synopses, or summaries, of thousands of books online and this provides yet another source of support in making a choice of reading material.

Online booksellers

Amazon was one of the first successful dot com businesses, and made popular the 'customer review' and 'customer ratings' features which are now commonplace. Customer reviews, rather than the more formal and literary review found in print, can offer some support in choosing a book. Readers may also be encouraged to post their own review as part of the read-write process.

Search engines are also powerful ways of locating books easily, by author or keyword, and this may be much easier and more convenient than using a library or book shop. Some retail websites offer the opportunity to 'look inside' the book to see the size of print, quality of illustrations, contents page listings, etc., thereby offering an opportunity to try before you buy and, again, an incentive to read.

Online buyers can check prices from different suppliers and decide whether to buy new or second hand. They are therefore able to easily access a range of potential book purchases at reduced cost. Some Internet-based booksellers provide a feature with similarities to social bookmarking (described in the previous chapter), in which readers are informed that 'Customers Who Bought This Item Also Bought …'. These recommendations, generated by a computerised system that checks and compares prior sales, serve a commercial function. However, they can also benefit the reader by giving him or her ideas which may extend the range of their reading materials.

Visiting an author's website

Readers are often curious to know more about an author, and this may lead to further reading. Many authors have official websites which contain a diverse range of features and material, such as biographies, excerpts, news, links to associated websites, multimedia content (including streaming and downloadable interviews and podcasts), photo galleries, and opportunities to purchase titles and subscribe to newsletters and mailing lists. All these features may add to the pleasure and fun of reading.

Bringing the author closer: online chat and email

Many websites also offer options for contacting the author, either directly or via the publisher, agent or personal assistant, usually through email. A reader can ask questions and receive answers in a public forum. One popular feature is 'online chat', such as used on websites like Richard and Judy's Book Club (**http://www.richardandjudybookclub.co.uk/**). Online chats are publicised in advance through the site and other means such as on television, radio, or in a newspaper or magazine. Users then visit the site at a specified time and are able to communicate directly with an author about a book or related enquiry in real time. Some online chat facilities encourage users to send in questions in advance of the event in order to give the author time to prepare an answer. A transcript of the chat may be archived, perhaps stored with other interviews with the author, so it can also be accessed by others at a later date.

These additional features and the personal nature of the interaction between reader and author can be very motivating. The material may provide an interesting insight, shed light on something unnoticed in a book, or acknowledge the influence of other books and sources of inspiration on the author, which the reader may then want to follow up.

Books enhanced through links on the Internet

Increasingly, books are being published which contain links to Internet content, such as multimedia supplements, games, competitions and complementary information. This works to enhance and support the reading experience by engaging the reader more deeply and encouraging him or her to solve puzzles through gathering clues in the book and then exploring the Internet-linked content for more information.

Novel ideas, with the help of the web

Rather than supporting reading for pleasure, online book experiments, such as 'BookCrossing' ('Where ink hits the road'), are helpful in encouraging reading for pleasure. BookCrossing is a method of sharing books in a fun and novel way. Members of the BookCrossing community 'release' books by leaving them in specific places. With clues/instructions from the previous owner, other members are able to locate and then read the 'released' book. There is then the potential for the finder to become a more active member of the BookCrossing community: he or she may contribute to forums, hunt for new 'released' books and 'release' some books of their own, all of which encourages wider reading and reading for pleasure.

Fan fiction

'Fan fiction' (also known as 'fanfiction', 'fanfic', 'FF' or 'ffic') is a loosely-defined term to describe fictional material that is written by people who are admirers of a book, film, cartoon, comic, television series or computer game. These stories are increasingly crafted and can run to 40 webpages or more. Writers of fan fiction use the characters or settings depicted in their favourite film, book, etc. and bring them to life in new stories that extend or depart from their original depictions and actions. It can be a very satisfying creative experience for a fan and amateur writer to bring back to life, for instance, a popular character 'killed-off' in the original narrative, and to explore what they would do next, having been resurrected.

Most fan fiction is read by fellow fans of a particular book, film, etc., which means that the writers can assume their readers have a similarly good knowledge of the original. This encourages reading for pleasure because it brings together, in a social and (usually) supportive environment, readers and writers with a shared interest. Fan fiction has a real potential to draw reluctant readers towards reading. For example, an enthusiastic fan of the *Terminator* films may have little interest in reading, but may feel compelled to find out what happens to characters after the events portrayed at the end of the most recent sequel, and therefore may come across some relevant fan fiction while browsing the Internet. It is certainly possible that the fan may enjoy the experience of reading the story so much that he or she will read further fan fiction, or other (print-based) novels.

All of the above offer a great variety of ways in which reading can be enjoyed in other ways than simply working through a book from cover to cover, and those who work with reluctant or inexperienced readers may find it helpful to encourage some experimentation with these opportunities.

Book clubs and forums
- Recommendations can reassure readers suffering 'information overload' and lack of confidence
- Provides recommendations trusted more than blurbs on back covers
- Allows reading to become a social activity

Different perspectives
- Ability to access diverse points of view that shed new light on reading

Social
- Making connections
- Learn what others think about a book
- Share with others what you learn online
- Connect with other readers and feel like you are part of a group

Reading and writing reviews
- Widely-available and accessible
- Guidance to help uncertain potential readers choose a title
- Opportunity to write and share views

Building on 'Traditional Reading'

Online booksellers
- Discount prices can be enabling for many readers
- Commonly feature helpful recommendations, ratings and reviews
- Search features and listing options increase usability and access to sought-after books

Visiting an author's website
- Extends and enhances the reading experience
- Rich and diverse content: biographies, news, multimedia, excerpts, links, retail, subscriptions

Bringing the author closer
- Opportunities for email correspondence with author enlivens the pleasure of reading
- Online chats enable users to converse with authors about their writing in real time
- Transcripts from online chats, and interviews in other media, are often archived for readers to follow up at their own convenience

Fan fiction
- Extends reading by bringing new life to literary/fictional characters and settings
- Sharing and inspiring others, especially new readers

Novel ideas online
- Innovative sites such as BookCrossing encourage reading for pleasure through fun, challenging book-related activities
- Joining a community and sharing reading

Books linked online
- Reading experience becomes more interactive
- Extends and enriches the content of a printed book

Notes

1. *2008 Kids and Family Reading Report – Reading in the 21st Century: Turning the Page with Technology* (Scholastic and TSC 2008)
   http://www.scholastic.com/aboutscholastic/news/kfrr08web.pdf (accessed March 2009)
2. ibid p31
3. ibid p4
4. ibid p12
5. http://royalsociety.org/bookspage.asp?id=6958 (accessed November 2008)
6. http://www.facebook.com/group.php?gid=2345834133

Chapter 5

Removing barriers to reading

Previous chapters have looked at resources and ideas to persuade reluctant readers to engage with reading, whether on screen or in print. In this chapter we consider that group of readers for whom reading presents a physical or sensory difficulty, and look at the two main ways in which barriers to reading can be removed. One is the use of devices other than a PC to access reading material, and the other is the way in which electronic text can be adapted to make it more accessible, which has benefit for people with a wide range of disabilities. We interviewed a number of people whose stories demonstrate these benefits. Some of their names have been changed.

Rudi has multiple sclerosis, and although he can read the text, he cannot turn the page unaided. Ivy is in her eighties and is increasingly housebound, reliant on others to bring her magazines and books. Simon has sight problems and finds reading very tiring: 'I now need magnifiers to do crossword and Sudoku puzzles and can only do so much before my eyes start "swimming" in the print.'

Markos has dyslexia. At the age of 35 he has never finished a book but enjoys reading about celebrity chefs. He knows their life stories and is a regular visitor to TV programme websites and message boards. He sets the text size to 'largest' on his Internet browser and uses a program called Screen Ruler (**http://www.screenruler.co.uk**) to mark out one line of text at a time to stop the print blurring.

what Dominique has been through.

Each week, she has a meeting with her, where they discuss any problems she is having - from claiming

nutritious food, and identifying and pursuing training or work opportunities. Our aim is to give them all the tools they need to live independent and fulfilling lives.

Example of the Screen Ruler Program being used to single out individual lines of text.

Doreen has learning disabilities and will never be a fluent reader in a conventional sense. Nevertheless she is adept at reading symbols and has recently become fascinated by the poisonous frogs in Costa Rica on the Symbol Rainforest website (**http://www.widgit.com/rainforest/**).

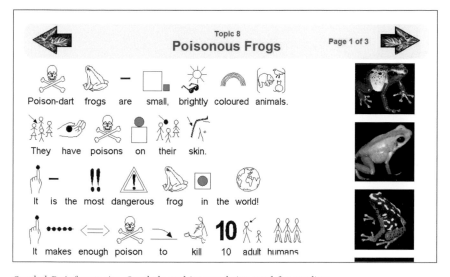

Symbol Rainforest site. Symbols and images being used for reading.

Here are the stories of some people who have found their own way of reading for pleasure, along with some suggestions of useful software, hardware, peripherals and downloads to make reading a little bit easier. Many of the previous features of the Internet that can add to the reading experience are also available to those who find the physical experience of reading a traditional book inaccessible or less convenient than electronic text.

> 'Reading' does not have to be just text. Look at symbols and images especially for learners who have a limited knowledge of English or who have learning disabilities.
> Text on a screen can be easier to read than text on a page. Change the font size colour or use a program like Screen Ruler to single out individual lines of text.

Adrian's story

Adrian is blind. Although he is a very experienced and knowledgeable user of assistive technology, he still finds that reading can be a frustrating experience. While everyone appreciates the odd classic now and then, it's no substitute when your mates are queuing up at midnight for the latest *Harry Potter* or picking up a rare and exotic cookbook in the charity shop for 20p. According to a recent report by the Royal National Institute for the Blind (RNIB), less than 4 per cent of books are produced in alternative formats, so the choice is always going to be limited.

'Most of my reading for pleasure falls into one of two categories – mindless action thrillers of the spy or military type or travel books. Of course, with an audio book you can't skim read – you can't whizz past the diary entries or letters pages, or skip easily to the start of the next chapter. The reader makes a world of difference in an audio book: an average title can be lifted by the right voice, or a work of art trashed by a poor recording.'

'I source virtually all my leisure reading material from audible.co.uk where you can purchase and download audio books for burning to CD, transferring to a portable device including MP3 player or mobile phone, or just listen at your PC. I mostly use a Zen stone MP3 player – the controls are as simple as you can possibly imagine. At £20, it's one of the cheapest MP3 players on the market, it's half the size of a pack of chewing gum and holds more audio than I can possibly listen to in a month. An unabridged audio book in the high street could cost between £30-£50 but a subscription service such as Audible really brings down the price, offering one title a month for £8 or two a month for £15.'

Useful technologies

Daisy (Digital Accessible Information System)
(http://www.daisy.org.uk) is an increasingly popular way of
publishing digital talking books using high-quality synthetic
speech or human voice. With a Daisy book, a reader has a measure
of control and can speed up or slow down the reading, move easily
from chapter to chapter, heading to heading and page to page, put
in bookmarks and choose whether to read or ignore footnotes.

There are different types of Daisy players. Many digital audio
players which can play MP3 files will be able to play a Daisy book
but will not offer all the navigation features. Daisy books can be
borrowed on disc from the RNIB's Talking Book Service, bought
from their Book Site or downloaded to a computer from The
BookStream book club (http://booksite.rnib.org.uk/eDelivery/).
For an annual subscription of £50, readers can 'borrow' up to five
books at any one time and keep them for an indefinite period.

The Talking Newspaper Association of the UK
(http://www.tnauk.org.uk) offers more than 200 digital
newspapers and magazines in a range of audio and full-text
formats.

There are several free **screen-reader programs** and more are
coming out all the time. Because they speak the text aloud, they
can support not only visually impaired readers but also early
readers, those with dyslexia and those for whom English is an
additional language. Some screen-readers just read text that has
been cut and pasted, other programs will read webpages as well as
Word documents and some can convert text to MP3 files. Here is a
selection of programs currently available:

> Thunder (http://www.screenreader.net/)

> Readplease (http://www.readplease.com/)

> Microsoft Reader
  (http://www.microsoft.com/reader/downloads/default.mspx)

> Read The Words (http://www.readthewords.com/)

> Browsealoud (http://www.browsealoud.com/page.asp)

> WordTalk (http://www.wordtalk.org.uk)

For blind readers, there are a number of specialist programs such as Zoomtext (http://www.sightandsound.co.uk/) or Jaws (http://freedom-scientific-jaws.software.informer.com/) but users need training to get the most from these packages. Dolphin (http://www.yourdolphin.com/dolphin.asp) provides specialist technology for people who are blind or visually impaired including:

> Supernova – a combined screen reader and screen magnifier with full Braille support;

> Hal – a screen reader with Braille support;

> Lunar – a screen magnifier for partially sighted users; and

> LunarPlus – a screen magnifier with speech support.

Good contacts

Abilitynet (http://www.abilitynet.org.uk/)

Claro software (http://www.clarosoftware.com/)

Becta (http://www.becta.org.uk/)

TechDis (http://www.techdis.ac.uk/)

Listening Books (http://www.listeningbooks.org.uk)

Calibre (http://www.calibre.org.uk)

RNIB (http://www.rnib.org.uk)

Audible (http://www.audible.co.uk)

Inclusion website (http://inclusion.ngfl.gov.uk)

Look for downloads and FREE software to support learners who have poor sight. Many older learners will fall into this category.

One in five people aged over 65 in the UK have a sight loss that significantly affects their daily life.[1]

Phyllis' story

Phyllis was born in 1916 and confounds most of the stereotypes of older people and computers. Now in her nineties, Phyllis has mobility problems and some hearing loss.

'I have lived through a period of real expansion from the beginnings of the radio right through to computers. I did use computers at work, although in those days they took up a whole room. Now a little laptop has more power than those old computers.

'I like reading but if the weather permits, I would rather be in the garden. At the moment I am reading lots of online articles about hydroponics, finding out how to grow cuttings from plants without soil. I have *Gardeners World* magazine every month and get their online newsletter too which has lots of offers. I belong to their reader panel so I take part in some of the surveys.

'The web gives me easy access to information I want. I have been tracing my family history and can go back to 1861 on my father's side. I am still trying to find my way round the BBC site, Who Do You Think You Are?. I also use commercial sites but I don't like them so much as they are forever asking you to buy credits to see information and sometimes you are not sure if you have got the right person.

'I do like Ancestry.com because they give you a fortnight's free viewing. After that you have to pay but you get access to more information. I find some of the census returns are hard to read so I use the Magnifier in Accessories to make them bigger. I've found some really interesting information. My father fought in the Boer War and at the time of the 1901 census he was not listed with the rest of the family in Coventry because he was in a holding camp in Catterick awaiting discharge.

'As well as helping me with my hobbies, the computer keeps me in touch with friends. I've just got a webcam so when I contact people through Messenger we can see one another and talk, as well as sending typed messages – all very clever. I now have an email "penpal" in Johannesburg. I really enjoy reading her news. We have never met but I do have an invitation to pop over to South Africa for Christmas!'

It is not always necessary to buy expensive specialist software. Try downloads and cheap or free text readers.

Useful technologies

For many readers, once they've mastered using a computer, they can use the standard settings and pursue a whole range of interests. For others – particularly older readers whose sight is failing – there are a number of accessibility options that can help, many of them free and found in desktop environments.

Settings for the mouse, keyboard and display can be changed in the Control Panel:

> 'Display' lets you change screen colours, size and definition to make the desktop and documents easier to read. It is straightforward to change the icon size too.
> 'Mouse Properties' contains options that let you change the mouse controls, the size of the pointer and whether you want it to leave a trail. Experiment with the Double-click speed on the Buttons tab, the Scheme on the Pointers tab, and Speed on the Motion tab. If the mouse is a major problem, try a Tracker Ball or other input devices. Inclusive technology (**http://www.inclusive.co.uk/**) provides a range of devices.

Keyboards can also be adjusted to help those with fine motor control:

> StickyKeys is an accessibility feature designed for people who have difficulty holding down two or more keys at a time, for example control+ alt+ delete.
> FilterKeys can make the computer ignore repeated key strokes. This is useful for users with any form of tremor.
> SerialKeys is an accessibility feature designed for people who have difficulty using the computer's standard keyboard or mouse, and lets them use an alternative input device.

Computers often give sound warnings or alerts – which is helpful if your hearing is acute. For those who need extra support:

> SoundSentry provides a visual warning instead of a sound message; and

> ShowSounds instructs programs that usually convey information only by sound to provide all information visually, such as by displaying text captions or informative icons.

> Do not make assumptions about older learners. They are not necessarily technophobic!

> Some older learners had IT skills from their working days.

> Some learners will find that mouse alternatives such as a Roller Ball or Pen Mouse offer greater precision. This may well benefit people who have a tremor which may be caused by drugs, including some prescribed medication, alcohol or certain medical conditions.

Good contacts

Microsoft (**http://www.microsoft.com/enable**)

AbilityNet (**http://www.abilitynet.org.uk/**)

RNIB (**http://www.rnib.org.uk**)

Although the Internet has something for everyone, there are a number of sites now catering specifically for older people. For example, OPIN (the Older People's Information Network) (http://www.opin.org.uk) is a free information service for people over 50 in the Coventry area.

There are also lifestyle sites, such as Lifestyle 60 (**http://www.lifestyle60.com/**) which is for those who are retired or approaching retirement. It has sections on events, UK and overseas property, free dating, travel, money, health, cooking, gardening and pets.

Learners from South Cheshire Collge

Jonathon White is a lecturer at South Cheshire College. He asked a group of students on Entry Level courses about their reading. Some learners can read text independently and use the web to search for information about their hobbies, but others need more support.

Jessica uses a **DynaVox DV4** to communicate and is in the first year of an Independent Living Skills course. She is a very pictorial learner, using icons and symbols. She uses Google Image Search on the web to look for photos.

Nicky is a first-year Entry Level student doing Business and Administration who likes to read about historical events, especially the First and Second World Wars. 'I often use the Internet at home to find information. I change the size of the font in Internet Explorer, via View then Text Size. I have it on Largest. I also copy and paste the text into a program called ReadPlease (**http://www.readplease.com**) which reads it out loud. I use Ask Jeeves, Google and Wikipedia but I like BBC History the best.'

Andrew uses the computer at college to play games. 'In IT I use Widgit Communicate: Webwide (**http://www.widgit.com/products/webwide/index.htm**) It reads the words to me. It can also give me a symbol for a word, which helps. When I am not in my lessons, I play *Deal or No Deal* and *Tetris*. We have our own website called Our Space (**www.s-cheshire.ac.uk/New_scc/spotlight/entrylev/home.htm**).'

James enjoys reading about sport: 'I read about Man Utd FC at home on the computer. I find out about the different players and the manager. I also read about WWE wrestling to find out about the different wrestlers. I also use my computer at home for games like *Football Manager 2008*. I read about players and buy and sell them. I use MSN at home and I chat by typing to friends and read their replies. I say "Hello" and "what RU up to?". I like email. I use Microsoft Outlook at college. I use Hotmail at home.'

Many of the students read *eLIVE*, a free online monthly magazine which can be accessed from the Symbol World site (**http://www.symbolworld.org/**). Some of them have also become regular contributors to the magazine too. *eLIVE* contains news, film reviews and a community section with a career interview –

everything from being a film maker to a worm farmer! Often there is a profile of a country, with interesting facts and holiday photographs. Recent features have included the Chelsea Flower Show, the beast of Exmoor, Victorian circuses in Leamington Spa and the use of hero rats to detect landmines in Africa.

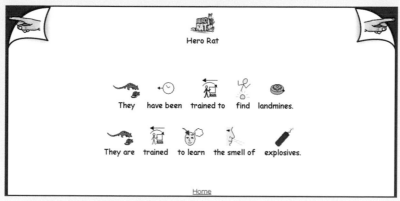

eLIVE magazine article on hero rats

Each page is switch accessible and contains just one or two sentences with symbol support. The site is also speech enabled so the text can be read aloud.

> 'A beginner reader is not a beginner thinker' is one of the tenets of skills for life work. This is especially true of those learners who have learning disabilities.
> Find stimulating materials which meet learners' interests, not their reading level.
> Is there symbol support?
> Check if sites are accessible to switch users too.

Useful technologies

> Simplified keyboards have fewer options and so are less confusing.
> Overlay keyboards have a range of options to help learners access the computer in different ways.
> Switches come in a variety of shapes and sizes and can be operated by any controlled movement of the body.

Good contacts

> The British Institute of Learning Disabilities (BILD)
  (**http://www.bild.org.uk**) is a charity that provides
  information, publications and training and consultancy services
  about learning disabilities for organisations and individuals.
> Inclusive Technology
  (**http://www.inclusive.co.uk/index.shtml**) has information as
  well as assistive products, and also offer a range of reading
  materials in conjunction with Gatehouse Books.
> Mencap acts for people with a learning disability and their
  families. (**http://www.mencap.org.uk/**)
> Home Farm Trust provides training in Person Centred
  Technology. (**http://www.hft.org.uk**)
> Widgit (**http://www.widgit.com**) produces a range of
  universally recognised symbols which are attached to words in
  order to help make them clear.
> Symbolworld (**http://www.symbolworld.org**) presents the
  latest news, features, recipes and film reviews in symbol format.
  A range of symbolised books and a symbol-supported web
  browser are available from the Widgit website.

Zoe's Story

Zoe has dyslexia. As she finds it very tiring to read black print on a white background, she has tried to find alternatives to printed books whenever she can.

'I really got into using the Internet when I was studying art. I found it hard to read about artists because I used to get sore eyes. Now I try to use the computer as much as possible. I am signed up to several RSS feeds. One of the best is PostSecret (**http://postsecret.blogspot.com/**), an online community art project where people send in their secrets. I get a summary on a Sunday morning and for me it's even better than reading the Sunday papers. Often I use the TechDis toolbar (**http://www.techdis.ac.uk/index.php?p=1_20051905100544**) which lets me change the size and colour of text to make it easier to read. I like reading blogs – not just famous people but stuff written by ordinary people too. My friend Julie is a great traveller and I log onto her blog (**http://restless-cinnamongirl.blogspot.com**) fairly often. This year she has been in Sri Lanka, Japan and Spain and it's great reading first-hand accounts about these places.

'I am going to get a Sony reader from Waterstone's. I love a good crime novel and I really like "Morse" because I have seen them on television so I find it quite easy to visualise the stories and characters. Waterstone's is launching lots of the Colin Dexter books as e-books for £4.76 each. The reader will hold over 150 books, which will be far more than I will ever read! Although I won't be able to change the colours of the "paper" and print I will be able to change the font size and can listen to the text as an MP3 file through headphones. That will really help because often I read so slowly that I just give up.'

E-readers

The Sony Reader is one of the first generation e-readers. It is smaller than a hardback, weighs 260g, can store up to 160 e-books and has a battery life equivalent to approximately 6,800 continuous page turns. The makers believe it comes close to a traditional book page in size and format and, unlike computer screens it can be read in direct sunlight or at angles of up to nearly 180 degrees. Readers can choose to have the text in three different sizes. Toby Young, author of *How to Lose Friends and Alienate People*, believes they will have many benefits both for readers and the publishing industry:

> *'The great thing about electronic books is that in the long run they will benefit writers, creating an easier way to enable first-time authors to get their work in front of the public. That will be a revolutionary change!'*[2]

Useful technologies

Text-to-speech software is good for those who want to have text read aloud. There are a number of free programs, as described in the section on visual impairment, but users may benefit from commercial programs such as ClaroRead (http://www.clarosoftware.com/) or Texthelp Read and Write (http://www.dyslexic.com/read-write-gold).

Good contacts

> Project Gutenberg (**www.gutenberg.org**) now has over 25,000 downloadable books available free of charge.
> Dyslexic.com offers information, product reviews and the *Assist Newsletter* which discusses issues of interest to people who have dyslexia.
> Audio downloads for the Man Booker 2008 'longlist' of 13 titles can be downloaded (**www.themanbookerprize.com/news/audio**). The Man Booker awards have also gone into partnership with the mobile site GoSpoken. Now readers can download audio extracts of the six shortlisted titles onto their mobile phones free of charge by texting MBP to 60300. (Outside the UK, enter **gospoken.com/a/mbp08** into the mobile web browser.) Readers can also use their phone to download the full audio book or have a hard copy delivered direct to their homes. The cost will be added to their mobile phone bill.
> The Reading Pen Oxford Dictionary (**http://www.scanningpens.co.uk**) contains over 240,000 words and definitions, and hundreds of phrases.

Changing the colours of text and background can make reading easier, as can changing the spacing between lines. Useful keyboard shortcuts include (ctrl A = select all; ctrl 5 = 1.5 spacing; ctrl 2 double spacing).

> TechDis has a free User Preferences Toolbar which gives tutors and learners a simple way of changing the appearance of just about any webpage. Users can choose different colour schemes including high contrast, serif and non-serif fonts and a zoom function that magnifies the webpage.

Michael's Story

In July 2006 Michael Garton attempted to become the first British solo climber to reach the summit of Trollveggen. At 3,600 feet this is the tallest vertical rock face in Europe.

He broke his neck after falling 120ft and nearly died of hypothermia before being rescued by the Norwegian Air Force. Michael was unconscious for 12 days and spent three weeks in an intensive care unit in Norway before being flown back to the Northern General Hospital in Sheffield. Initially, he was paralysed from the neck down but has started to regain some movement in his arms.

'Prior to my accident I did plenty of reading, mainly instructional material such as climbing and mountaineering guides, books on predicting weather and so on. In addition, I read chemistry journals and textbooks for university and work. I couldn't call myself a big reader because I was pretty active and so didn't get the time.

'I definitely read more now as I have more time. Since my accident I have been using Dragon Dictate voice-activated software, to access the computer. I use a Bluetooth headset and have a multimedia projector attached to my laptop which can project onto a wall or onto the ceiling if necessary. I navigate by voice commands, "Page Down" etc. If I am reading a newspaper online I can often just say a keyword from a headline such as "Iraq" or "Barack Obama" and it will go straight to that story.

I can combine this with a number of innovative mouse options to facilitate rapid navigation around a computer. My favourite is a tube operated by mouth with a "suck and puff" mechanism that operates the left and right click. Others include giant tracker pads and infrared technology using a reflective spot on the nose.

'I do read fiction and whilst some material is available online, I prefer to struggle with actual hard copy. If I can, I buy the larger format as it is easier to hold open and I stack things on my desk to achieve a manageable height. It is difficult to turn the pages but I find it is possible with a bit of patience.'

Useful technologies

> The Gewa Page Turner will turn pages of books and magazines up to 5cm thick. It can be used by people who are lying down or sitting up so it is ideal for people who are confined to bed (http://www.possum.co.uk/). Trackballs/Joysticks are alternatives to mice which do not move around the desk and can be operated with two hands, if necessary.
> Michael's story shows that text can be made accessible through technology, support and training. There is no single 'right' solution and some people will need expert assessment if they are to be able to navigate effectively around a screen.
> Projecting text onto a wall can make it easier to read.
> Some people like to read a newspaper online but still prefer the traditional format for 'books.'

Good contacts

> Dragon Dictate and Naturally Speaking (http://www.nuance.com/)
> The CALL Centre has information on using Dragon (http://callcentre.education.ed.ac.uk/Research/Speech_ Recog_PRA/DragonSR_PRB/dragonsr_prb.html)

Notes

1. http://www.rnib.org.uk
2. Thompson, J. *The Big Question: Do electronic books threaten the future of traditional publishing? The Independent*, 24 July 2008 http://www.independent.co.uk/lifestyle/gadgets-and-tech/features/the-big-question-do-electronic-booksthreaten-the-future-of-traditional-publishing-875724.html

Chapter 6

Conclusion

Last year saw the publication of a report, *Information Behaviour of the Researcher of the Future*,[1] commissioned by the British Library and Joint Information Systems Committee (JISC), and carried out by researchers at University College London (UCL). The report looks at academic disciplines but many of its findings are also equally relevant to discussions about the impact of technology on reading for pleasure. UCL conducted a longitudinal study over five years looking into the behaviour of the so called 'Google Generation' which they defined as anyone born after 1993. They found that most users skimmed sites, looking at a maximum of three pages before 'bouncing out'. In other words, they flicked from one site to another and looked at a multiplicity of resources rather than drilling down into one particular set of webpages. The researchers typified this as 'searching horizontally rather than vertically'.[2] They also discovered that many characteristics which they had felt typified the behaviour of the younger generation were also apparent in other age groups: 'Everyone exhibits a bouncing, flicking behaviour…Power browsing and viewing is the norm for all'.[3]

It seems that rather than savouring every word, users are spending time skimming and scanning, reading for gist, reading in a non-linear way, and generally being more selective in what they read and what they skip.

> *The average times that users spend on e-book and e-journal sites are very short: typically four and eight minutes respectively. It is clear that users are not reading online in the traditional sense, indeed there are signs that new forms of `reading' are emerging as users `power browse' horizontally through titles, contents pages and abstracts going for quick wins. It almost seems that they go online to avoid reading in the traditional sense.*[4]

These 'new forms of reading' are linked to many of the activities discussed, with the enormous choice of reading material being one reason for this changing behaviour. Readers increasingly have to make active choices about what to read and what to reject. In the past the choice was simpler as reading materials were by and large controlled by businesses, publishing houses and the government. Indeed, one can think of the trials of the 1960s such as *Lady Chatterley's Lover* and *Last Exit to Brooklyn* or the more recent example of Peter Wright's *Spy Catcher* being banned in the UK. Such censorship and control is unthinkable today. Now with the Internet there is much more freedom for both authors and readers. This 2008 report also confirms our discussion on the changing nature of the distinction between reading and writing:

> *The emergence of social web sites is changing the nature and fabric of the world wide web: we have moved from an internet built by a few thousand authors to one being constructed by millions. Social networking is of particular interest to librarians and publishers because it is part of a wider trend: users creating and posting content for themselves, blurring the age-old distinction between information producers and information consumers.*[5]

Reading for pleasure can be promoted and enhanced by the opportunities afforded by this wealth of content and ways it can be accessed. Whether skimming or scanning, for less confident readers, the range of content available, and the personalised nature of discovering it are strong attractions of reading online, either instead of, or as well as the traditional print-based experience. E-Books and text on mobile devices present a new means of reading which, for many, can improve access to a pleasurable reading experience. New forms of reading should not be seen as inferior, but instead, the positive role that technology can play should be acknowledged and used to help people find the enjoyment and benefits that reading for pleasure can bring.

Notes

1. *Information Behaviour of the Researcher of the Future* (2008) University College London. **http://www.bl.uk/news/pdf/googlegen.pdf** (accessed March 2009)
2. ibid p4
3. ibid p8, citing CIBER research work package IV
4. ibid p10
5. ibid p16

Glossary

An **aggregator** is a piece of software that pulls together various RSS feeds and collects them in one place to give the reader a personalised, up-to-date briefing on the latest changes in a range of chosen websites, e.g. a news reader, which streams current and breaking news items to a subscriber.

A **blog** (a contraction of the term 'Web log') is a website, usually maintained by an individual, with regular entries of commentary, descriptions of events, or other material such as graphics or video. Entries are displayed in chronological order, with the most recent listed first.

Blogels and **Blovels** are serial narratives produced through blogs. They are written as short episodes and updated regularly.

Blogosphere is a term to describe the sense of public opinion which becomes apparent through the works of the whole community of bloggers

Cyberspace – a metaphorical space not linked to any government or country or nationality where all computer text, images or other media can be said to exist.

Digital fiction commonly involves hypertext, sound, image and video content to support and enliven screen-based text. It can be a very interactive medium.

Distributed narratives/ email fiction – Stories are told through a series of emails exchanged among the characters. Instead of reading these emails in a book, they are regularly sent to a reader's inbox as part of a regular instalment.

Folksonomy is the process of attributing key words, descriptors or tags to content. These key words are generated by readers and users of the content as much as by experts, so it is seen as a 'bottom up' way of categorising information.

A **forum** is a discussion site. It can be viewed by the public but only those who have registered can contribute. They can submit posts which are public messages. These may be on one particular topic or thread.

Hypertext and **hyperlinks** are letters, words and images which you can click on to take you to other pages on the Internet. They are often in blue writing or have a finger icon to indicate that they are live links.

Instant messaging (IM) and **chat** are technologies which allow real-time text-based communication between two or more participants. It may run via an Intranet or across the Internet so participants are not necessarily in the same country but type messages backwards and forwards to one another in real time. It is a very instant form of communication.

Podcasts are a series of audio or video files which can be accessed or downloaded from the Internet to portable media players and personal computers.

RSS stands for 'Really Simple Syndication'. RSS is a 'feed', a regular stream of updated information from chosen websites, which you can receive on your computer, meaning that the most up-to-date information on your favourite websites is 'fed' to you, without you having to spend time and effort periodically checking those websites individually. RSS makes use of a code that frequently scans the content of a website for updates and then broadcasts those updates to all those subscribed.

Social Bookmarking is the practice of saving bookmarks to a public website and 'tagging' them with keywords, thereby sharing your preferences with others. To create a collection of social bookmarks, you register with a social bookmarking site, which lets you store bookmarks, add tags of your choice and designate individual bookmarks as public or private. Some sites periodically verify that bookmarks still work, notifying users when a URL no longer functions.

Social networking means building online communities of people who share interests and/or activities, or who are interested in exploring the interests and activities of others. Most social network services are web based and provide a variety of ways for users to interact, such as email and instant messaging services.

Thread messages on a bulletin board or an email forum are usually grouped both chronologically and by topic. A set of messages on a topic is known as a thread.

Twitter Fiction – Twitter only allows 140 characters or less so it can be used to produce short works of fiction.

Web 2.0 is an umbrella term for social networking sites that includes wikis, blogs, social bookmarking, podcasts, RSS feeds, etc. These enable users to append, create and comment on content and participate in creating content for a site.

A **wiki** is a collaborative website to which individuals can contribute their content, knowledge and understanding to specific pages about a particular topic. Depending on the administrative control of the page, a wiki may operate as a completely open system where anyone can contribute or as a more controlled system where contributions may only be made by registered users of the wiki.

Other useful resources

▶▶ The Vital Link (**http://www.literacytrust.org.uk/vitallink/index.html**) is run by The Reading Agency in partnership with the National Literacy Trust and NIACE. Its aim is to provide a bridge between Skills for Life providers and local libraries so that reading for pleasure becomes a key part of the curriculum. Libraries can kickstart a host of lively and fun reading activities which can motivate students or engage new learners. There are lots of useful resources for emergent readers such as the range of Quick Reads titles (**http://www.quickreads.org.uk**) including ten new books published on World Book Day 2009 by authors such as Josephine Cox.

▶▶ There are online toolkits and case studies (**http://www.vitallink.org.uk**) which demonstrate ways of working with emergent readers in partnership with libraries and ideas for integrating Quick Reads into teaching at www.vitallink.org.uk and www.quickreadsideas.org.uk as well as resources and activities.

▶▶ NIACE (**http://www.niace.org.uk**) has recently launched a new website, Reading for Pleasure (**http://www.readingforpleasure.org.uk**) with a wide range of resources for tutors and learners. Funded by DIUS, these materials were produced in partnership with the Vital Link and Quick Reads. There are resources and ideas for use in family learning, literacy and numeracy, as well as resources for continuing professional development (CPD).

▶▶ Try out the Six Book Challenge – Libraries, working with local learning providers, are encouraging adult learners to read six books and keep a diary showing their progress and thoughts. Over 40 prisons ran the challenge. Organisations can obtain information leaflets, registration cards, reading diaries, bookmarks and certificates from The Reading Agency. (**http://www.sixbookchallenge.org.uk**)

▶▶ The Vital Link is also encouraging men to get involved in reading to their children as reading has fewer male role models. To encourage those who are not confident or enthusiastic readers there are some suggestions ranging from The Five Minutes collection (**http://www.literacytrust.org.uk/vitallink/fiveminutes.html**) with books by Nick Hornby and Jeremy Clarkson as well as children's classics such as *Funnybones* and *Spot the Dog*. A Vital Link with Parents project in

2007 promoted these books through libraries, children's centres and family learning workers. In Warrington, local role models such as a policeman, a fire fighter and a real-life Mr Universe led a series of story times.

▶▶ Booktrust (http://www.booktrust.org.uk/Home) is an independent national charity dedicated to promoting books and reading to people of all ages. Booktrust is responsible for a number of national reading promotions, literary prizes and creative reading projects. They also provide the content for several other sites.

▶▶ The short story site (http://www.theshortstory.org.uk/) has guidance for readers and writers and details of awards. There are reviews and downloads, a chance to read or listen to good new short fiction. Another of their sites is a guide to London via the novelists, poets and playwrights who have lived there over the centuries (http://www.getlondonreading.co.uk/). It features the Google Book Map, where users can click on areas of London to find out about some 400 fiction and non-fiction books that are set in the capital or feature London in some way.

▶▶ The Campaign for Learning devoted its National Learning at Work Day on 22 May 2008 to the National Year of Reading, helping organisations to run activities to celebrate reading, increase motivation and develop skills. (http://www.campaign-for-learning.org.uk/)

▶▶ RaW (http://bbc.co.uk/raw) is the BBC's biggest ever campaign that aims to help adults across the UK read and write better. You can now access information, quizzes and much more content to help improve your reading and writing on your mobile. It has six mini episodes of BBC Scotland's ongoing drama, *River City*. It also has the RaW Reader that lets you read or listen to the first chapters of all 12 of the Quick Read books. Quick Reads are short, fast paced books by bestselling writers. They are perfect for people looking for an introduction to reading or regular readers who want a bite-sized book. The 2009 titles were published on World Book Day, Thursday 5 March 2009, at just £1.99 each.

▶▶ First Choice Books (http://www.firstchoicebooks.org.uk/) has books from sport to humour, love to crime. You can also let others know what you think about a book you've read by rating it and writing a comment.

▶▶ myBSLbooks.com (http://www.mybslbooks.com/) – a range of popular children's books, available for the first time free online in British Sign Language. This site offers deaf children and their families the chance to enjoy signed stories.

▶▶ Reading for Life (http://www.readingforlife.org.uk/) takes forward all the lessons learned from the National Year of Reading in 2008.

Appendix 1 Choosing a blog to use with learners as a learning diary

An extract from Starter for One, an ESF supported project that investigated the use of blogs as learning diaries.

Ease of set up
How easily and quickly can a learner set up a blog?

Are there costs attached?

Can learners individualise the design of their blog?

- Access to a web address is essential – most blogs require a registration with an email address and are activated through clicking on the link in a confirmation email.
- Select a blog that does not require completion of a great deal of personal detail in the registration process – it is preferable to complete a personal profile at a later time when the use of the diary is understood.
- Select a free blogging tool unless there are circumstances that mean a customised solution is required. The disadvantage of free tools is advertising and pop-ups.
- Most blogs have a choice of design templates, allowing the learner to select background colours, layout etc. Look for templates that provide maximum space for content and demonstrate and recommend those at the early stages.

Clarity of interface
How comfortable are the learners with using the Internet?

- Advertising and pop-ups can be very distracting for some users, especially those who have less experience of using the Internet.
- Select a blog with a WYSIWIG (What you see is what you get) interface. Look for a simple interface for uploading media files, such as a media 'library'.

Features
Can learners upload a full range of media files?

- Check the functionality of the tool to ensure images, audio files and video can all be uploaded in a similar manner.
- Check the file types that can be uploaded, e.g. MP3, jpeg etc. Match this with the equipment and software that will be used to create the diary entries.
- Check the maximum file sizes and encourage learners to keep multimedia entries short, and to edit their content carefully.